AAT Foundation Certificate in Accounting
Level 2
Work Effectively in Finance

Second edition 2017

ISBN 9781 5097 1239 7

British Library Cataloguing-in-Publication Data

A catalogue record for this book is available from the British Library

Published by

BPP Learning Media Ltd
BPP House, Aldine Place
142-144 Uxbridge
Road London W12 8AA

www.bpp.com/learningmedia

Printed in the United Kingdom

Your learning materials, published by BPP Learning Media Ltd, are printed on paper obtained from traceable sustainable sources.

Welcome to BPP Learning Media's AAT **Passcards for Work Effectively in Finance.**

- They **save you time**. Important topics are summarised for you.
- They incorporate **diagrams** to kick start your memory.
- They follow the overall **structure** of the BPP Course Book, but BPP Learning Media's AAT **Passcards** are not just a condensed book. Each card has been separately designed for clear presentation. Topics are self contained and can be grasped visually.
- AAT **Passcards** are **just the right size** for pockets and bags.
- AAT **Passcards focus on the assessment** you will be facing.
- AAT **Passcards focus on the essential points** that you need to know in the workplace, or when completing your computer based exam.

Run through the complete set of **Passcards** as often as you can during your final revision period. The day before the assessment, try to go through the **Passcards** again! You will then be well on your way to completing the assessment successfully.

Good luck!

For reference to the Bibliography of the AAT Work Effectively in Finance Passcards please go to: www.bpp.com/learning-media/about/bibliographies

Contents

The BPP **Question Bank** contains activities and assessments that provide invaluable practice in the skills you need to complete this unit successfully.

1: The role of the financial functions

Topic List

Functions within an organisation

The financial functions

Contribution to business objectives

The legal framework

This chapter introduces the role of financial functions within an organisation. It explores the various ways in which those individuals in financial roles contribute to business objectives.

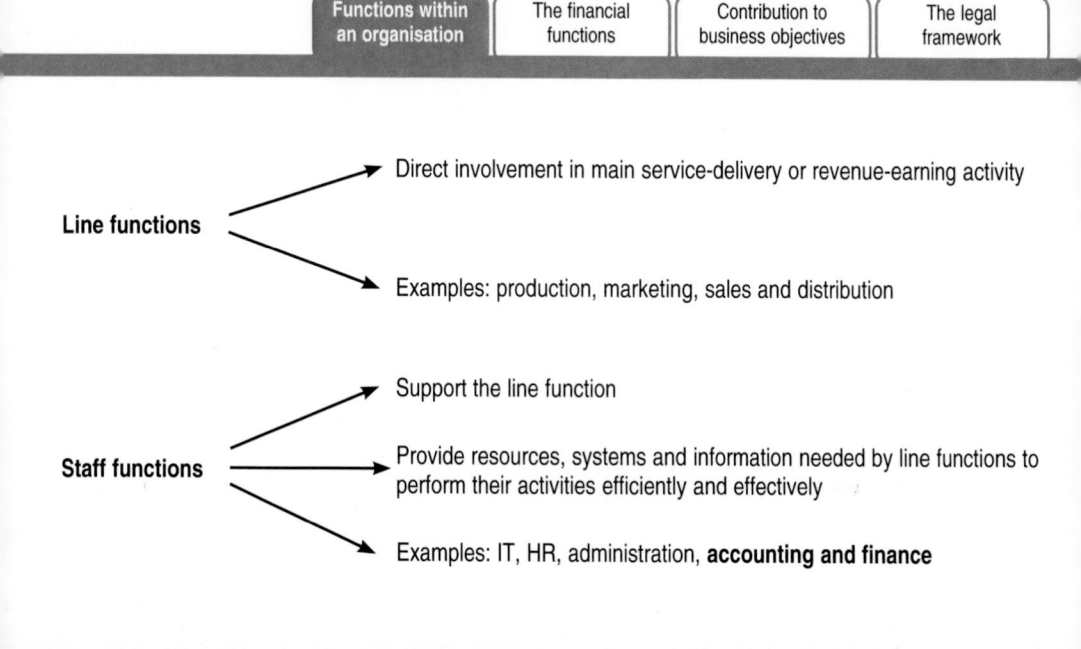

Line functions

→ Direct involvement in main service-delivery or revenue-earning activity

→ Examples: production, marketing, sales and distribution

Staff functions

→ Support the line function

→ Provide resources, systems and information needed by line functions to perform their activities efficiently and effectively

→ Examples: IT, HR, administration, **accounting and finance**

The data used to prepare management accounts and financial accounts are the same. The differences between these accounts arise because the data is analysed in a different way.

Management accounts

- Distributed internally for use within business
- Management decide on way in which they are presented
- Help management in planning, control and decision making
- Look at both past and future data
- Not legally required to prepare them
- Include both financial and non-financial information

Financial accounts

- Used for external reporting
- Legal requirement for limited companies to prepare them
- Look at past data only
- Usually include financial information only
- Detailed results for a defined period

1: The role of the financial functions

Payroll is concerned solely with payroll processing eg calculation of gross pay and deductions; preparing payslips; making returns to external agencies (such as HMRC, pension providers); paying employees; preparing payroll statistics.

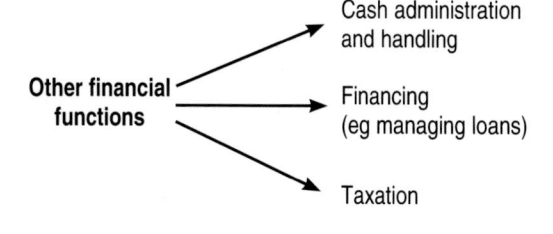

Other financial functions

- Cash administration and handling
- Financing (eg managing loans)
- Taxation

Financial functions are **service and support** providers. Their main role is to provide complete, accurate and timely information on the financial implications of the line functions:

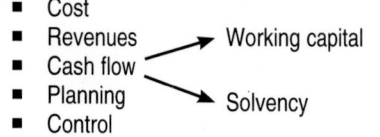

- Cost
- Revenues
- Cash flow
- Planning
- Control

→ Working capital

→ Solvency

Accounting and financial functions make an important contribution in these key areas:

- **Smooth running and efficiency of the business** – achieving objectives with the minimum use of resources eg budgeting and long-term plans used as benchmarks; actual performance details to compare to budget; identify areas where performance and efficiency can be improved.

- **Working capital and solvency of the business** – managing working capital used in the day-to-day running of the business eg provides information on cash flow (cash in and out of the business); planning for cash shortages by obtaining finance; ensures the business is solvent (ie able to pay its debts).

- **Legal compliance of the business** – to be able to comply with legislation so that the business benefits from a positive reputation for compliance and so avoid or minimise legal penalties (such as fines).

Compliance with the law is important because:

- The law is there to protect people from loss and suffering, and ensure minimum acceptable standards of management.
- There may be financial penalties (eg fines, compensation) and operational penalties (eg loss of licence) for non-compliance.
- Non-compliance can damage the reputation of the organisation and its ability to attract investors, customers and staff.
- Non-compliance can lead to burdens and costs of corrective action, closer scrutiny in the future and so on.

For an organisation in the UK, the main sources of law are UK statutes (or Acts of Parliament), EU Directives issued by the European Union, and regulations made under those laws.

2: The organisational framework

Topic List

Organisation structure

Reporting lines

Policies and procedures

This chapter looks at the organisational framework, including reporting structures and the various organisational policies and procedures that may apply to your work.

The formal structure of an organisation can be illustrated by an **organisational chart**. An organisational chart for a small electrical firm follows.

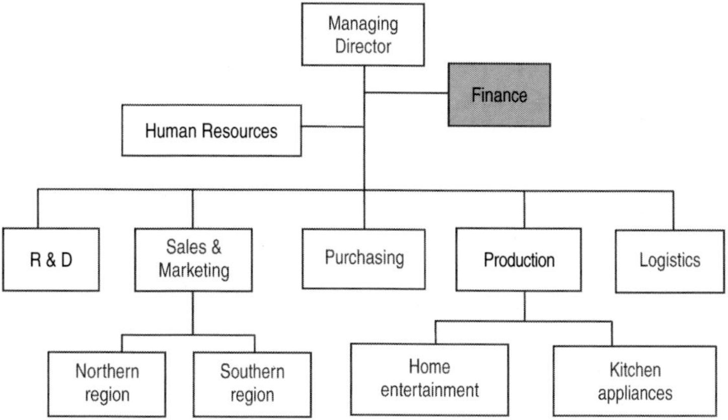

Organisation structure is the 'shape' of an organisation.

- Different units eg functions, departments, geographical, product types
- Power, authority and responsibility – chain of command
- Lines of communication and co-operation

```
                      Managing
                      Director
                         |
                         +--------------------+
                         |               Finance
            Human Resources
                         |
   +---------+-----------+-----------+-----------+
   |         |           |           |           |
  R & D   Sales &    Purchasing  Production   Logistics
          Marketing                   |
              |                       |
        +----------+           +-------------+
        |          |           |             |
     Northern   Southern     Home        Kitchen
     region     region    entertainment  appliances
```

A chart for a finance function could be as shown below:

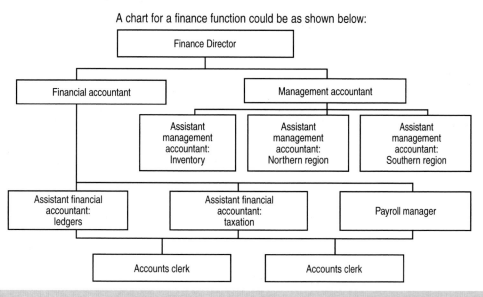

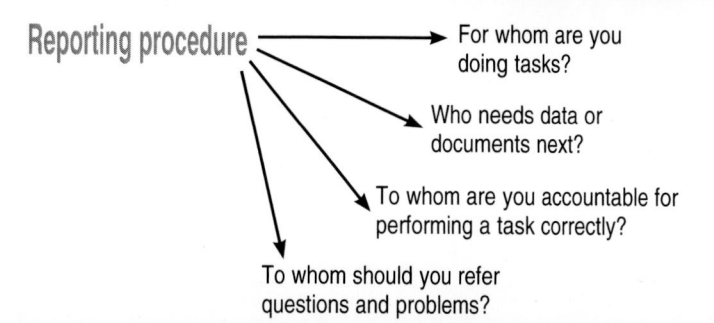

Reporting procedure

→ For whom are you doing tasks?

→ Who needs data or documents next?

→ To whom are you accountable for performing a task correctly?

→ To whom should you refer questions and problems?

Reporting lines for a given job and task

Line manager: eg in the organisation chart on page 13, the accounts clerk reports to the assistant financial accountant who reports to the financial accountant who reports to the finance director.

Project manager: eg if working on a specific project, there may be a project manager designated for that project.

Policy

is a statement of how an organisation works and expects activities to be carried out.

Examples

Equal opportunities policy; health and safety policy; working hours policy; clear desk policy; confidentiality of information policy; data security policy

Procedure

is a standard sequence of steps or operations necessary to perform an activity.

Examples

Handling of cash receipts; authorisation of payments; secure storage of data; timesheets; keeping information confidential and not releasing it to unauthorised persons

Deadlines

must be adhered to.

Examples

Payroll preparation; accounts preparation; financial statements

Notes

3: Personal skills

This chapter and the following one will develop the knowledge and skills needed to perform effectively.

Topic List

Effective business communication

Message content and presentation

Business language

Numeracy skills

| **Effective business communication** | Message content and presentation | Business language | Numeracy skills |

Working effectively in finance is fundamentally about the effective preparation, giving and receiving of information. All of this requires effective communication – with colleagues, with other departments and with stakeholders outside the organisation.

Information communicated should be:

- Complete
- Accurate
- Timely
- Fit for purpose

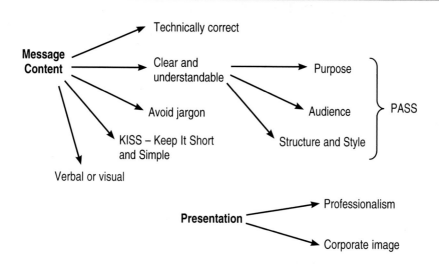

Message Content
- → Technically correct
- → Clear and understandable
  - → Purpose
  - → Audience
  - → Structure and Style
- → Avoid jargon
- → KISS – Keep It Short and Simple
- → Verbal or visual

Purpose, Audience, Structure and Style → PASS

Presentation
- → Professionalism
- → Corporate image

Business language

must be courteous, businesslike and professional.

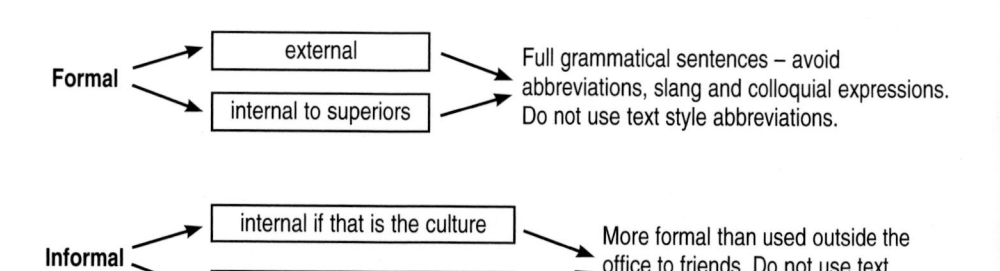

Formal → external → Full grammatical sentences – avoid abbreviations, slang and colloquial expressions. Do not use text style abbreviations.

Formal → internal to superiors →

Informal → internal if that is the culture → More formal than used outside the office to friends. Do not use text style abbreviations.

Informal → appropriate to a work colleague →

This should be revision from *Basic Accounting*. Make sure you understand and can use the following techniques:

- Addition
- Subtraction
- Multiplication
- Division
- Fractions
- Percentages
- Rounding
- Averages
- Proportions
- Ratios

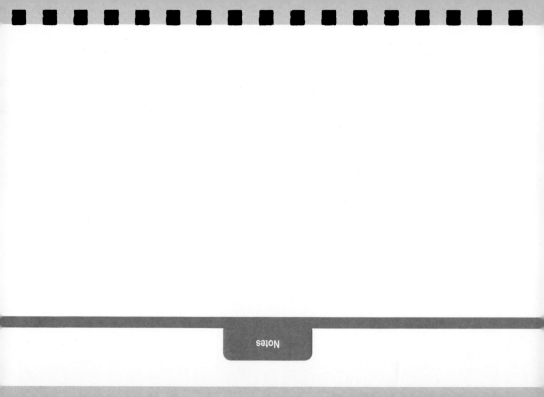

Notes

4: Presenting information

Topic List

Choosing formats

House style, guidelines and policies

Informal business reports

Using diagrams and charts

Business letters, memos and emails

This chapter develops the skills learnt in the previous chapter to enable you to produce informal business reports, letters, emails and memos to a professional standard.

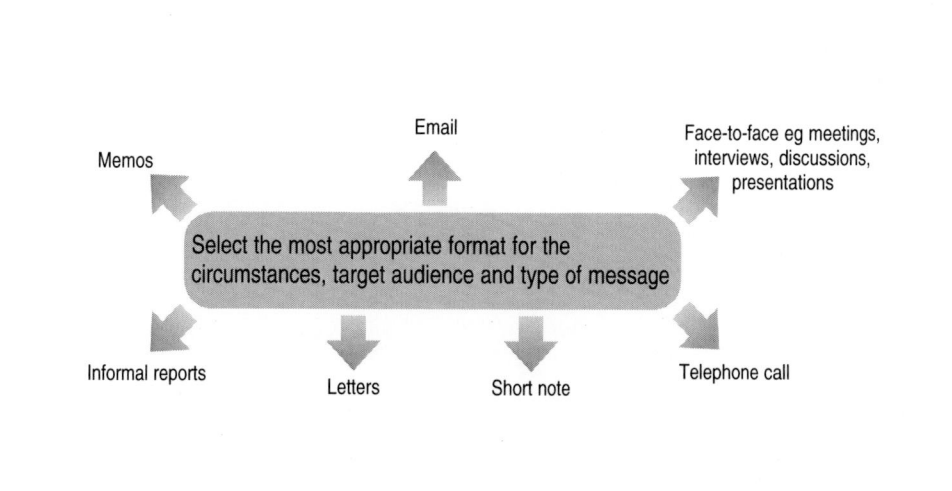

Email

Face-to-face eg meetings, interviews, discussions, presentations

Memos

Select the most appropriate format for the circumstances, target audience and type of message

Informal reports

Letters

Short note

Telephone call

Is there a communications policy? If so it will provide guidelines on how to use (not abuse) tools such as the telephone and emails. There may be restrictions as well eg not using the internet for personal purposes.

House style includes the use of standard letterheads; how letters and memos are laid out; email signatures. Your organisation may have proforma formats ready for use.

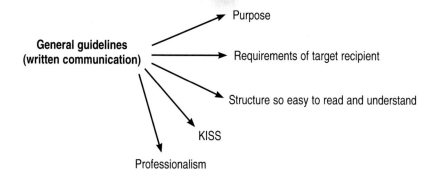

General guidelines (written communication)

→ Purpose

→ Requirements of target recipient

→ Structure so easy to read and understand

→ KISS

→ Professionalism

Reports

- Routine
- Occasional
- Special
- Professional or non-professional

Content of a report

- Title
- Executive summary
- Introduction
- Main body
- Conclusions
- Recommendations
- Appendices

Reports will usually be communications that are intended to initiate a decision or action by the person or group receiving the report. Eg control action or planning decisions.

PAY ATTENTION!

Beware of over-using jargon and technical terms.

Keep vocabulary, sentences and paragraphs as simple as possible.

Consider the level of detail that will be relevant to the users.

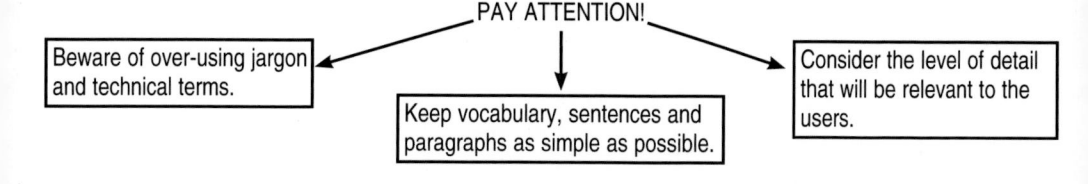

TIMELINESS ⟶ As with all information, a report may be of no use at all if it is not produced on time.

Planning a report
■ Who is the user?
■ What type of report will be most useful to him/her?
■ What exactly does the report user need to know?
■ How much information is required, how quickly and at what cost?

Making your report easier to read
■ Using suitable sections or sub-headings
■ Is the subject of the report too technical for the users?
■ Do I have a clear introduction and clear conclusion?

In preparing a report, visual aids may be helpful.

- Tables
- Bar charts
- Pie charts
- Line graphs

Letters

are most likely to be used when communicating with someone outside your organisation.

Information letters

are simple ways of presenting a report or details of events or products.

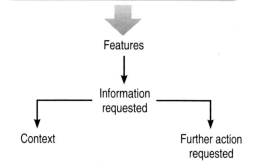

Features

Information requested

Context

Further action requested

Emails

can be used in the same way as memos or for external communications where signatures are unnecessary.

Memos

provide internally the same function as a letter does in external communication. It can be used for any kind of communication that is best conveyed in writing, such as reports, brief messages or notes.

Advantages of emails

- Speed
- Economy
- Efficiency
- Security
- Can attach documents and reports

5: Working independently

Topic List

Time management

Setting priorities

Planning aids and deadlines

You need to be able to show that you can plan and organise your work effectively and prioritise your activities.

TP03-5321-024

Routine tasks

- Open post
- Deal with emails
- Pay suppliers' invoices
- Prepare sales invoices
- Prepare bank reconciliation

Unexpected tasks

- Prepare report for manager
- Cover for sick colleague
- Help colleague to meet a deadline

Priorities

Urgent and important tasks

|

Not urgent but important tasks

|

Urgent but not important tasks

|

Not urgent and not important tasks

Scheduling

If important tasks appear you must be prepared to change priorities and the order in which tasks are carried out.

Once you have a list of priorities, **schedule** tasks by determining when they will be done.

Planning aids

- To do list
- Diary or timetable
- Planning schedules and charts
- Action plans

Deadline

- If a deadline is unlikely to be met it must be reported immediately
- Manager may be able to change deadline/organise assistance/lighten your existing work load/provide additional resources

Seeking assistance

- Must recognise that assistance is required
- Identify assistance/resources required
- Negotiate the assistance
- Co-ordinate the assistance

6: Working as part of a team

Topic List

Team working

Interpersonal skills

Conflicts and grievance procedures

You will often have to work as part of a team and need to be able to communicate with that team as well as with other employees and managers.

Features

- Agree/understand objectives of team
- Be aware of resources available to team
- Working methods set by team leader
- Work schedules set by team leader
- Integrate work with other members of team
- Be prepared to provide assistance/support to other team members

Advantages

- Additional resources
- Inspiration
- Motivation
- Communication
- Synergy

Disadvantages

- Personality clashes
- Decision making takes longer

Interpersonal behaviour is behaviour between people. It includes:

- Interaction between people: two way processes such as mutual assistance and support
- An individual's behaviour in relation to other people: assertiveness, empathy etc

Interpersonal skills include:

- Rapport-building: establishing relationships
- Persuasion/influence
- Assertiveness ■
- Negotiation
- Conflict resolution
- Empathy: understanding others
- Oral/non-verbal communication
- Appropriate roles and relationships

Assertive

Clear, honest, direct communication which respects the rights of self and other: not passive, not aggressive.

- Asking clearly and openly for what you want
- Saying 'no' without being defensive
- Receiving feedback/criticism objectively
- Giving criticism constructively

Types of conflict

Conflicts due to:

- Personality
- Working style
- Status
- Work demands
- Competition
- Unfair treatment
- Hurtful treatment

Disagreement

It is important that colleagues should be able to disagree but still maintain good working relations.

Escalation

Unresolved conflict and dissatisfaction may need to be taken to higher authority (escalation).

Grievance procedures

If the matter is serious, a more formal approach may be needed. A grievance is a formal complaint and an organisation should have written grievance procedures to deal with this.

7: Developing skills and knowledge

Topic List

Systematic approach

On-the-job training

Off-the-job training

Development

This chapter covers how an individual can develop themselves through learning and acquiring new skills and knowledge.

A systematic approach to training

Stage One: training needs analysis

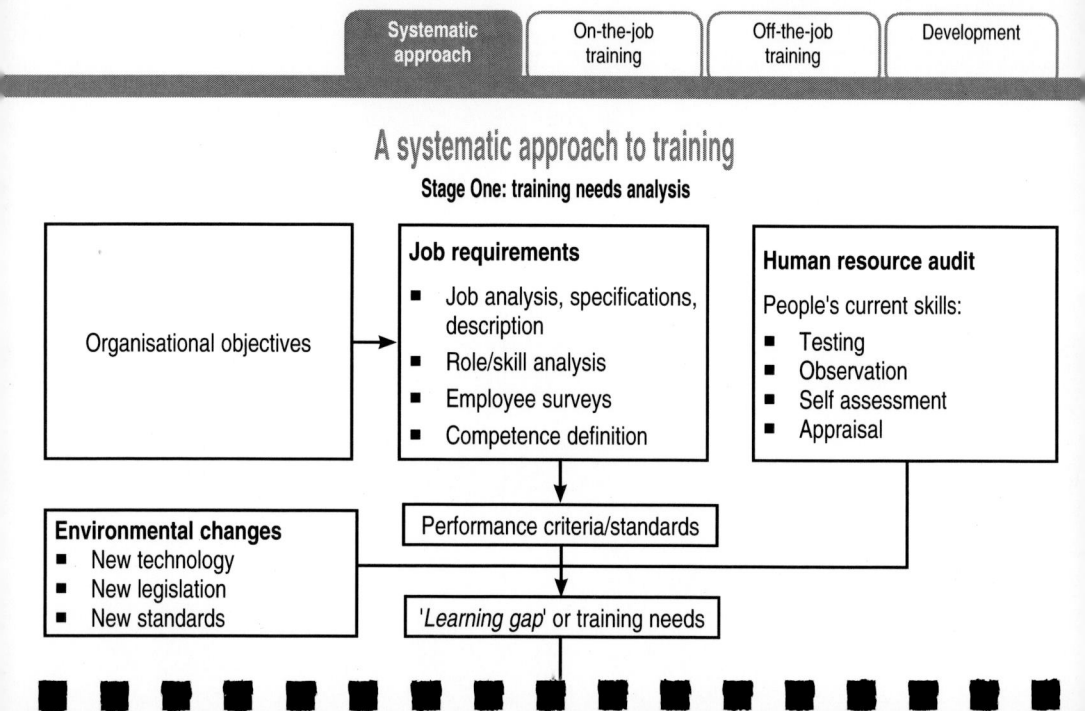

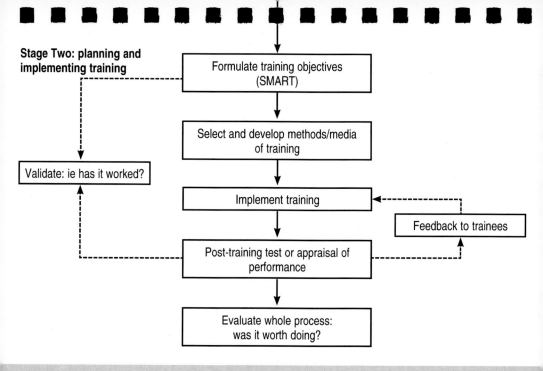

Stage Two: planning and implementing training

Formulate training objectives (SMART)

↓

Select and develop methods/media of training

↓

Implement training ← Feedback to trainees

↓

Post-training test or appraisal of performance → Feedback to trainees

Validate: ie has it worked?

↓

Evaluate whole process: was it worth doing?

7: Developing skills and knowledge

On-the-job training methods include:

Method	Outcome
'Sitting with Nellie'	Observation/imitation
Job instruction	Demonstration/explanation
Coaching	Guidance, advice, teaching
Job rotation	Gaining work experience
Temporary promotion	Gaining management experience
'Assistant to' positions	Shadowing managerial work
Committee/project work	Exposure to other functions
Apprenticeships	Mix of off and on-the-job
One to one	Instruction

Induction training is the introduction of new recruits to the job, work place and work group. It begins an on-going process of development.

On-the-job methods

+ Relevant to job skills
+ 'Fit' with job context
+ Establish work relationships
+ Suit active/pragmatic learning styles
− Depends on training skills of fellow workers/supervisors
− Risk, pressure, distraction of 'real' work context
− May train unhelpful methods/culture
− Requires tolerance of error

Off-the-job training methods include:

- Training room instruction
- Lectures/taught classes
- Case study analysis
- Role plays
- Simulations/in-tray exercises

} In-house training facilities **or** external training providers – accessed via training leave, day release, evening classes etc

- Visits and tours
- Outdoor training

} Off-site training events

- Distance or open learning
- Computer/video-based learning

} Flexible, use-anywhere training packages, webinars

Off-the-job methods

- \+ Allow experimentation without risk, pressure of work
- \+ Away from interruptions, distractions of work
- \+ Can allow for own-pace study
- \+ Suit theoretical learners
- − May not relate directly to task or job context
- − Less immediate motivation and feedback for learning
- − Does not suit all learners
- − Can create anticlimax on return to work

'Development' is a wider concept than training, although training provides learning and educational experiences for development.

Skill/competence development:

Acquiring job-relevant knowledge, skills etc through education and training.

Career development

Identifying career aspirations and planning progression through:

- Gathering different experiences
- Using mentors and role models
- Accepting opportunities and challenges

Personal development

Seeking wider learning experiences, to meet self actualisation needs and goals.

Employability development

Acquiring a portfolio of experience/competence that enhances mobility/value in the labour market.

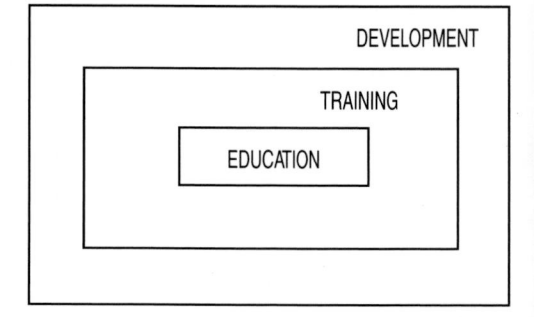

8: Understanding ethical and sustainable values

Topic List

Ethics

Conflicts of interest

Business ethics

Sustainability

Organisations are embedded in society and must respond to public concerns about ethical behaviour and sustainability. The AAT has its own ethical code for members.

Behaviour in society is regulated by the law, rules and regulations, and in some cases by ethical codes.

AAT Code

The AAT has a Code of Professional Ethics. The advice for a member is:

- Avoid even the appearance of a conflict of interest
- Be objective and act in the public interest
- Keep sensitive information confidential
- Be straightforward and honest in all dealings
- Maintain professional knowledge, behaviour and skills
- Act within the spirit as well as the letter of the law

Illegal/Unethical

Lawful

Meet regulatory obligations

Ethical

Why should accountants behave ethically?

- Laws and regulation
- Upholding of professional standards and qualities (personal/professional)
- Protection of the public interest

Enshrined in a 'Code of Ethics' or 'Code of Conduct'

Codes can be rules-based to account for every possible situation

or

Principles and frameworks to guide behaviour

The accountant:

IFAC – international body with its own code of ethics. AAT's is aligned:

F
u
n
d
a
m
e
n
t
a
l
s

- Integrity
- Objectivity
- Professional competence and due care
- Confidentiality
- Professional behaviour

via: reliability, responsibility, timeliness, courtesy, respect, equality

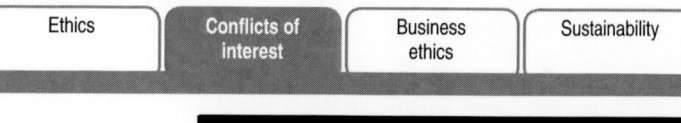

T
H
R
E
A
T
S

Self-interest

Self-review

Advocacy

Familiarity

Intimidation

Professional safeguards

- Entry requirements
- Training requirements
- CPD requirements
- Professional standards
- Professional monitoring
- Disciplinary procedures
- External review

Importance of independence

Independence promotes:

- Reliability of financial information
- Credibility of financial information
- Value for money of audit
- Credibility of profession

Safeguards in practice

- Peer review
- Independent consultation
- Partner/staff rotation
- Discussion/disclosure to audit committee
- Reperformance by another firm

Advocacy threat

Where accountants take client's part, act as their advocate or will only earn fees from client if successful outcome is achieved (contingent fees). Examples include provision of legal service and corporate finance advice.

Familiarity threat

- Family relationships between client and firm
- Personal relationships between client and firm
- Long association with client
- Recent service with client
- Future employment with client

Conflicts of interest

These can arise from accountants acting for clients with whom they are in dispute, eg over quality of work. It can also arise through disputes between two clients for whom accountants are acting.

Intimidation threat

- Close business relationships
- Family relationships
- Personal relationships
- Staff employed by client
- Litigation

An organisation's managers are collectively responsible for the conduct of an organisation's affairs: they have a **fiduciary responsibility** (duty of faithful service). This is often referred to as 'corporate social responsibility'.

How far do external pressures modify business objectives?

Stakeholder view

A business depends upon appropriate relationships with all groups who have an interest in what the organisation does. Each stakeholder group has its own objectives so that a compromise is required.

Consensus theory

Objectives emerge as a consensus of the differing views of shareholders, managers, employees, customers, suppliers and society at large but they are not all selected or controlled by management.

8: Understanding ethical and sustainable values

Sustainability

is a long-term program involving a series of sustainable development practices aimed at improving organisational efficiency, stakeholder support and market edge.

Duties of finance professionals

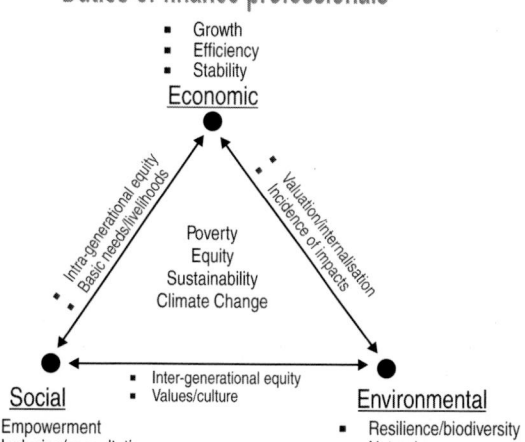

- Growth
- Efficiency
- Stability

Economic

Poverty
Equity
Sustainability
Climate Change

Intra-generational equity
Basic needs/livelihoods

Valuation/internalisation
Incidence of impacts

- Inter-generational equity
- Values/culture

Social

- Empowerment
- Inclusion/consultation
- Institutions/governance

Environmental

- Resilience/biodiversity
- Natural resources
- Pollution

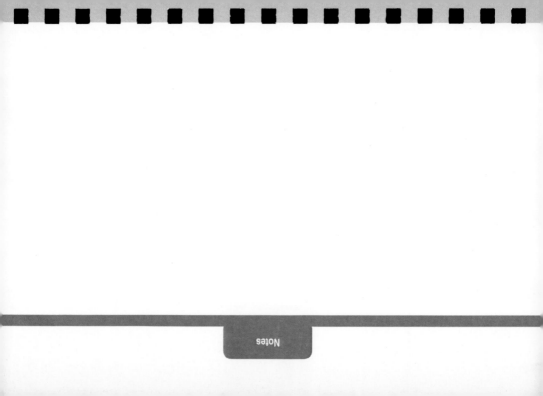

Notes

Notes

Notes

Notes

Notes

Notes